MW00720314

FINANCIAL TIPS
FOR A BETTER LIFE

FINANCIAL TIPS
FOR A BETTER LIFE

Simple and Effective Steps
to a Better Financial Future

Kenneth F. Robinson, JD, CFP®

Expert Publishing, Inc.
Andover, Minnesota

ISBN 10: 1-931945-49-7
ISBN 13: 978-1-931945-49-3

Library of Congress Catalog Number: 2006921226

Printed in the United States

First Printing: February 2006

10 09 08 07 06   6 5 4 3 2 1

Expert Publishing, Inc.

14314 Thrush Street NW
Andover, MN 55304-3330
1-877-755-4966
www.ExpertPublishingInc.com

DISCLAIMER

This publication is designed to provide accurate and authoritative information in regard to the subject matter covered. It is sold with the understanding that the publisher and author are not engaged in rendering legal, accounting, or investment advice, or any other professional service to the reader. If legal advice or other expert assistance is required, the services of a competent professional person should be sought.* The reader should take note that laws and rules applicable to their situation may change. It is the responsibility of the reader to seek further professional guidance whenever necessary. The author, publisher, and seller jointly and severally disclaim any warranty, express or implied, for any general or particular purpose, including any warranty of merchantability.

GUARANTEE

This book comes with a one-year money-back satisfaction guarantee. See complete details at The Kenneth Robinson Company website: *www.KennethRobinson.com*

* From a declaration of principles jointly adopted by a committee of the American Bar Association and a committee of publishers.

*For Ellen and Rebecca, more meaningful to
me than the richest treasure on earth.*

*And for my clients, from whom I've learned
so much they don't teach in financial
planning courses.*

CONTENTS

ACKNOWLEDGMENTS

My sincere thanks to the many people without whom this book would never have been completed.

To my colleagues in the Alliance of Cambridge Advisors, most especially to Bert Whitehead, Jo Anne Paynter, David Lentz, Pat Konetzny, Tedd Oyler, and Stewart Farnell.

To my colleagues in the National Speakers Association, particularly to Dawn Waldrop and Barb Wingfield, and to my colleagues in the Ohio Chapter, especially DaVeed, Greg, Linda, Jon, Larry, and Toni. The coffee's on me.

To Joy Oyler, for guiding me through the maze of obligations that accompany a project like this.

To my editor Barbara McNichol, for helping me understand how the written word is supposed to work; and to Sharron and Harry Stockhausen at Expert Publishing, Inc., whose patient, encouraging expertise has saved me untold hours of laborious effort.

To my entire family, most especially my wife, Ellen, and daughter, Rebecca, who tolerated and encouraged my taking the time to write this book.

It has been observed before that little is new in personal finance; there are simply new ways to convey current knowledge. My education in personal finance, both formal and informal, has come from a variety of sources. I have striven to acknowledge them where I have quoted the original ideas of others. Any omissions in this regard are unintentional. I would be greatly obliged to any who might identify a source I may have omitted.

INTRODUCTION

If your finances aren't in the shape you'd like, it's probably because you haven't taken the time–or had the time–to study the subject enough to feel confident about what to do next.

Many people fear taking charge of their financial lives. They worry that the process will be complicated, time-consuming, and hard to understand. Regardless of their level of education, some fear that the topic of personal finance may be too much for them.

And many of the books on the subject can actually make the reader feel even more overwhelmed. Some financial writing covers too much ground, inundates readers with too much detail, and leaves them feeling that any significant improvement means a large commitment of time and energy.

I believe that just a few words about personal finance—focused on the most fundamental choices that apply to working families—can be more valuable than the seemingly endless supply of advice available from the bookstore, the public library, and the Internet.

In fact, it's worth your while to merely improve your financial situation, even if you don't try to make it perfect.

Rather than writing yet another tome with all the details on every aspect of personal finance, this brief book calls to your attention a few important steps you can take to improve your finances. It is written for people who work for a living or who used to work for a living and are now retired. I've intentionally left out complex techniques useful only to multimillionaires.

How You Can Use This Book

Read every tip. Each one offers an individual step you can take or an idea you might adopt to help secure your financial future. You'll find space in the back for you to write action items to apply these ideas to your own life.

Specifically, you will find tips on general financial principles, saving and spending, debt management, U.S. income taxes, insurance, estate planning, college planning, and investing. Don't feel you have to apply each and every tip. Instead, find at least two or three tips on subjects important to you, and note how you can apply them to your life. These simple steps can make a significant difference in how you feel about money.

While some tips build on others, don't expect all these tips taken together to be enough to constitute a full financial plan. Yet, if you will just *begin*, applying even a few tips could help you create a new, more conscious, more intentional relationship with your money. You will feel you are finally managing your money *on purpose*. And when your money is in order, it's much easier to create the life you want. The less time you spend agonizing about finances, the more time you can devote to your family and friends, your community, and your unique human potential.

The moment you stop worrying about money, life gets better.

Great achievements are accomplished by adding together tiny improvements, one after another. Even the tallest building is built one brick at a time. As the Chinese philosopher Lao Tsu noted, "A journey of a thousand miles must begin with a single step."

So take a step. Apply one tip—just one—at first. Then, if you choose to, you can take more steps toward building a better financial future. As your financial situation improves, so will your contentment with life.

—*Ken Robinson*

GROUND RULES

These fundamental ideas apply to many facets of your financial life.

1
Keep money in its proper perspective.

Money has no inherent value of its own. It's a *tool* to help you do things that are more important than acquiring more money. Money management is best used to promote *a meaningful life*, filled with more joy, contentment, peace, love, and fulfillment than ever before.

2
Be yourself.

Don't worry about what your neighbors or co-workers do with their money. Their financial needs are different from yours. And what they tell you about their financial success usually gives you an incomplete picture. Focus on your financial situation and what works for you, not for someone else.

3
Live in the present.

If you've owned stocks, you may have experienced boom times like the late 1990s. But you can't get those days back by wishing, and no one knows if they'll ever come again. Don't worry about the unchangeable past or the unknowable future. Instead, focus on and work with the information you have today.

4
Stick to the basics.

Your personal finances can get highly complicated if you let them. Instead, keep everything as simple and straightforward as you can. Don't allow your finances to get any more complex than necessary to accomplish the job of building a better life.

SMART SAVING, SHREWD SPENDING

*Maximize your ability to live within your means.
This is the most crucial fundamental skill you need to
strengthen your finances.*

5
Try spending without using credit cards.

For just one week, leave your credit cards at home
and pay cash or write checks for everything. Doing
this requires a little planning, but it's not as incon-
venient as you might imagine, and you might be
inspired to make it a habit. As a bonus, you'll likely
spend less money. Remember, it's harder for most
people to part with actual cash than to sign for a
credit card purchase.

6
Don't make a budget—pay yourself first.

If you look at all your expenses to decide which ones to cut back on, you might feel a sense of loss, deprivation, and want. Doing this pits your feelings and your goals against one another—like constantly feeling hungry when you're on a diet. Instead, pay yourself first. Set a little money aside *as soon as you get paid* and before you pay the bills. Money that's put away tends to stay where it's put rather than get spent before the end of the month. You know this if you've ever found a dollar in a coat pocket or dresser drawer. This can be far more effective than merely hoping you'll have some extra money left at the end of the month.

7
Take your savings from your pocket money.

One of the most effective ways to pay yourself first is to reduce the amount of money you carry around. Take a little cash out of your wallet and set it aside every time you get paid. See if you can keep from spending it until your next payday. Don't worry about whether you'll have enough money for what you need. When you reduce your pocket cash—and limit your discretionary purchases to that cash— your *optional* spending gets curbed first.

8
Start small.

Like starving yourself to lose weight, saving tons of money all at once can be painful. Instead, start by saving between $5 and $50 from every paycheck. You can always raise the amount as time goes on.

9
Increase your savings little by little with every paycheck.

If you decide to save $5 every pay period, try to increase that amount by $5 with each succeeding one. If starting with $50 feels comfortable to you, try increasing your savings by $25 or $50 with each pay period that follows.

10
Congratulate yourself when you "hit the wall."

When you have increased your savings to a point that it feels like a strain, know that you haven't failed. Rather, "hitting the wall" shows how much you succeeded in the *previous* month. Chances are you've saved far more than ever before. Scale back your monthly saving to the last sustainable level, and make sure to continue building your savings account with ~~every future paycheck~~.

11

Put your savings where you can get it, but where you won't see it.

When you take cash out of your wallet, put it in an envelope in a place where you don't usually look for money, like a kitchen cupboard or a medicine cabinet. (My great-aunt used to wrap money in butcher paper, label it "frozen dough," and put it in the freezer.) If you put your savings in the bank, make sure it's in an account you don't normally use to pay your bills. You may want to open a new account strictly for savings.

12

Use direct deposit to make your savings automatic.

If your employer pays you by direct deposit, you can probably split the money between two or more bank accounts. In that case, direct a specific amount into a savings account, not into your regular checking account. This way, you'll automatically save money for yourself.

13

Set up a holding account for bills paid less often than once a month.

Instead of agonizing about how to pay that $600 insurance bill every six months, many advisors suggest you put $100 a month into a separate bank account. Saving for a large expense is less stressful than scrounging to pay that sum all at once. If you put away a portion of the required amount every month, you'll have the money when the bill comes—and you might have even earned a little interest on your savings.

14

Be honest with yourself about what you *really* need.

After you've paid for food, shelter, clothing, health care, and what's needed to keep your job or other income (work clothes, for example), almost every other purchase is negotiable. You may *want* to buy a lot of things, but remind yourself that your *real needs* are usually limited. When you take a second look at what you need versus what you want, you may happily decide against spending for certain extras.

15
Watch out for the phrase "it's only …"

Thinking "it's only a few bucks" can be a sign that you're trying to justify a purchase as being small and insignificant. But *everything* matters. It's often not the big purchases that get in the way of your ability to save, but the small habits that interfere with saving a little bit at a time, day by day.

16
Make a commitment to spend very consciously.

Get into the habit of being very suspicious of impulse purchases. Avoid sudden, knee-jerk spending. Take a moment to ask yourself if you really need, or even want, what you're about to buy.

17
Save your raises, bonuses, tax refunds, and other extra income.

Whenever you get a windfall—that is, when you receive more money than you usually take in during the pay period—put it into your savings account. If you already know how to live on your current income, you don't need that unexpected income to maintain your lifestyle.

18
Figure out how much working time it takes to purchase those "extras."

You may think that new computer will cost you $1,000. But if your take-home pay is $20 an hour, many financial advisors point out that this $1,000 actually costs you 50 hours of working time. Adopting this point of view may help you decide whether or not to make a discretionary purchase.

19
Find creative ways to experience things you enjoy for less money.

Instead of spending $1.50 or more for a cup of gourmet coffee, brew it at home for about 20 cents. Or take home a half gallon of your favorite flavor of ice cream for about the same cost as two or three servings at the ice cream parlor.

20
Preview books, movies, and music before you buy them.

Your public library can be a great resource for reducing your spending. Before you buy a book—whether it's a best seller or a hard-to-find title—borrow it from the library first to decide if you really want it.

The same goes for videocassettes, DVDs, and CDs that you can borrow free of charge.

21
Focus on value and function when deciding how much to spend.

You can spend between $3 and $15 to eat lunch at a restaurant, or you can spend $1.50 for lunch that you bring from home. Your homemade lunch is just as filling—and helps keep your wallet full, too.

22
Look for the extra benefits in your money-saving strategies.

Instead of buying breakfast at the local fast-food restaurant, eat at home and keep up with current events by reading the newspaper at the same time. Cancel extra cable channels and rediscover the pleasure of reading or chatting with your partner in the evening.

23
Give yourself permission to spend money on health and safety items, especially if they will save you money in the long run.

If paying a few dollars more for your children's bike helmets or sports equipment will keep them safer, it's money well spent. This also applies to buying a low-cost cellular phone for emergencies or that car repair you've been putting off. After all, the mechanic's bill will be much higher if you wreck your car because the brakes don't work.

24
If you need to replace your vehicle, buy a late-model used car.

New cars cost you thousands of dollars more than used cars, which may still carry the factory warranty. If you spend two hours inspecting a used car and having it reviewed by a mechanic, and then buy it for $3,000 less than you'd spend on a new car, you've just saved $1,500 an hour (probably a lot more than you earn at your job).

25
Pay cash for the next car you buy.

Instead of losing ground by paying the interest that goes into every car payment, gain ground by replenishing the cash you spent for the car. Instead of taking two steps forward and one step back because of your interest payment, you could be taking two steps forward plus *another* step forward by earning interest on your savings.

DEBT MANAGEMENT

We don't have to carry debt in our lives, but most of us do. Because the wrong kind can be so detrimental to your financial well-being, it pays to deal with debt as effectively as possible.

26
Review your credit reports annually and see that any errors are corrected.

U.S. residents are entitled to get one free credit report a year from each of the three major credit-reporting agencies. For details, go to www.annual creditreport.com, and get all three reports. Often the information found in them is different. Make sure all reports show an accurate credit history—have the reporting agency make any needed corrections.

27
Request credit reports for both spouses.

If you're married, be certain to get reports for each partner. You might be astonished to see how much your credit history differs from your spouse's. Review the reports for both spouses carefully.

28
Pay for one of the credit reporting agencies to give you your credit score.

Your credit score is a three-digit number that lenders, insurers, and others use to decide how they'll sell you services and at what prices. The higher your score, the better credit or purchase terms you qualify for. While you're reviewing your free annual credit reports, pay a few dollars for one of them to give you your credit score.

29
Borrow money only to pay for items that will last longer than the loan, and either tend to increase in value or bring you financial benefits that are greater than their cost.

Two examples of items that bring you value are your own home and your education. Financial planning pioneer Bert Whitehead calls these examples of "good debt" because they create positive financial effects, not the negative effects of consumer debt.

30
Only borrow when you can get favorable terms.

Home mortgages can present rare advantages like long-term fixed rates and interest payments that are often tax deductible. Loans for education may have similar features. Shop around for the best terms and rates.

31
Use credit cards *only* if you can pay them off every month.

Carrying credit card debt is the Achilles' heel of many a family's cash flow. Pay off the total amount on your credit card every month, so you won't get eaten alive by paying fees and interest charges.

32
Don't miss any opportunity to reduce your credit card debt.

If your total credit card debt stays at about the same level from month to month, you may have grown comfortable with a credit card balance of $500 (or $5,000 or $50,000). Be alert for, and take, small economizing steps that can help you pay down your debt, and thereby reduce the burden of interest payments with each passing month.

33
Give yourself enough time to pay off your credit card debt.

If you have credit card debt, you probably didn't accumulate it overnight. Give yourself time to dig out from under it. Many people take months or years to pay off their credit card debt.

34
Pay more than the required minimum on your credit card.

If you pay only the minimum amount required by your credit card company, a $5,000 balance on a typical card can take more than twenty-two years to pay and cost more than $11,000. Paying just 20 percent extra each month can knock this down to about fifteen years of payments, and can save over $2,000. Pay double the required minimum, and the card could be paid off in just under seven years, saving over $4,500.

35
Pay off the credit card that has the highest interest rate first to minimize the interest you'll pay over your lifetime.

Use this approach to pay the fewest dollars in interest over the long run. For example, a card with a $1,000 balance and a 20 percent finance charge costs you $200 over the course of a year, while one that charges 15 percent costs you $150—a savings of $50 if you pay off the card with the higher rate first.

36
Pay off the credit card with the lowest balance to free up your cash flow and help you feel you are making progress.

Use this approach to create more discretionary income in the short run by eliminating one minimum monthly payment. You may pay more interest over time on your cards collectively, but the relief of getting rid of even one card may be so motivating that it's worth the extra cost.

37
Don't carry a balance on more than one credit card.

Of course, it's best to pay off all of your cards in full every month. But if you carry a balance on more than one card, it can be easy to underestimate the total amount of your debt. For example, if your credit card bills show balances of, say, $5,900 and $5,925, you may see "$5,000 plus" on each account, and think you owe about $10,000. But you would actually owe almost $12,000. Cards for individual stores spread out your debt even further. If a store will accept your major credit card, consider cutting up the store card.

38
Don't transfer a balance to a card already carrying a balance from purchases.

Purchases often accrue interest at higher rates than balance transfers do. But card companies typically credit your payments to the balances with the *lowest* interest rates first. So the debt with the highest rate will typically stay on your card the longest. If you transfer a debt to a card that's already carrying a balance from purchases, you may end up paying the higher purchase finance charge for far longer.

39
Consider transferring all your balances onto one card with a low rate.

This can be a useful alternative if you'll need a long time to pay off your credit card debt. While you do have to watch out for balance transfer fees, you may be able to reduce your finance charges by moving existing balances to a card that will charge you less. Compare the finance charges, and figure out how much you would save during the time it will take to pay off the debt. Be careful, though, of teaser rates that may not last—try to find a card that will guarantee a low rate for the life of the balance.

40
Pay all your bills on time.

Suppose you're late paying a bill to Company A. Company B can use this information to increase the interest rate charged on your credit card from Company B. This is called *universal default* and is common in credit card agreements. On-time payment of *all* your debts—including your mortgage and car loans, for example—can be crucial in keeping favorable terms on your credit cards.

41
Ask your card issuer for a lower interest rate.

Sometimes you can get a lower rate just by calling the issuer and requesting it. It may help to mention a competing offer with better terms than your current card. Ask your current issuer to match the best terms you qualify for.

42
Make bigger payments on your consumer debt before paying off your mortgage.

The value of your home will typically rise over time, independently of how much is borrowed against it. If you have other debts that are more costly than your mortgage, pay them off first while making only the required payments on your house, especially if your mortgage is at a low fixed interest rate and if you can deduct the interest on your income tax return.

43
If you're in a hurry to pay off your traditional mortgage, keep this strategy in its proper perspective.

If your mortgage is a traditional 30- or 15-year fixed-rate loan, understand that the biggest benefit of paying it off is peace of mind, not financial savings. True, many people derive immense personal satisfaction and contentment from having their houses paid off. This seems to be a holdover from Great Depression era thinking when the motto may have been "don't lose your house to the bank." But many of us have better uses for our cash, especially if we're investing or paying down debt.

44
Use your after-tax rate to figure out the cost of your mortgage.

If you can deduct your mortgage interest from your taxes, figure out what percentage of interest the deduction saves you. For example, a taxpayer in the 25 percent bracket who benefits by itemizing deductions will pay only 5.25 percent after tax on his 7 percent mortgage. (7% – [25% x 7%] = 7% – 1.75% = 5.25%). Likewise, every $1,000 of interest would actually cost only $750, since the IRS doesn't tax the amount of the deductible interest. ($1,000 – [25% x $1,000] = $1,000 – $250 = $750).

45
If you're shopping for a new mortgage or refinancing an existing one, getting a 30-year fixed-rate loan is often your best choice.

If a 30-year fixed-rate mortgage is available to you, the peace of mind you gain from having a consistent payment likely outweighs any advantages of getting a variable-rate mortgage. This is especially true if you expect to live in the house for many years.

46
Don't roll your credit card debt into your mortgage, home equity loan, or line of credit.

At the least, wait until your credit cards have been cut up for six months or more before you do. You *must* learn to live without using credit cards before you refinance the balance. The problem isn't having to pay a high interest rate; it's the whole idea of buying now and paying later. Too often, you risk ending up with a bigger mortgage than before, *plus* a mountain of consumer debt.

47
Any time you pay off a loan, continue making the same monthly payment—to yourself.

To build your savings, pay the same monthly amount (from the paid-off loan) to yourself, putting it into your savings account. This won't hurt your lifestyle because you already know how to live without spending the amount of the loan payment on anything new. Saving this way is similar to banking your raises and windfalls instead of spending them as soon as you get them. (See tip 17.)

INCOME TAXES

Paying income taxes can be distressing.
But for many people, using simple, lawful techniques
can save thousands of tax dollars.

48
Bunch your itemized deductions for maximum tax savings.

If your itemized deductions usually come close to the standard income tax deduction amount, try what tax advisors call "bunching" your deductions into a single year. For instance, you could make two years of charitable contributions in a single year (actually giving more in one year, and then taking the next year off). This increases that year's allowable deduction. The next year, when you don't contribute to charity and don't have enough expenses to itemize, you'd take the standard deduction. By doing this, you get an extra benefit in the itemizing years and lose little (if anything) in the alternate years.

49
Bunch miscellaneous deductions to realize a greater tax benefit.

Miscellaneous deductions such as tax preparation costs and employee business expenses only show up as a benefit after they cost you more than 2 percent of your adjusted gross income (AGI). If you can combine those expenses (say, paying for continuing education every other year), you could increase the chance of getting a tax break instead of losing the benefit every year because the first 2 percent of AGI gets ignored. You might also apply this to out-of-pocket medical expenses, which have a threshold of 7.5 percent of AGI.

50
Avoid spending just to get the tax benefit.

If you are in a 25 percent tax bracket and you spend $100 on something you don't need merely to get the tax deduction, you might save $25 in taxes, but you've still lost another $75 to do it. Don't lose money chasing a tax deduction. Spend based on your needs and your lifestyle, not on how you can get a slightly larger refund.

51

Remember that saving on your income taxes won't force you to give up anything but time.

Reducing what you spend on, say, clothing probably means you'll have fewer outfits to wear. But to reduce your tax bill, you might not have to give up anything but some time, mostly for the proper record keeping. And you'll still be able to use the national parks, interstate highways, and other services that your tax dollars pay for.

52

Every November, project the amount you'll pay in income tax instead of waiting until April when taxes are due.

Avoid surprises that can show up when you only examine your tax situation just before the April 15 due date. Rather than looking through a rear-view mirror in April, look ahead in November at what you'll owe. This gives you time to carry out strategies such as changing your withholding and tax payments, selling securities so you can take advantage of capital gains or losses, or purchasing needed tax-deductible items before year-end.

53

Contribute to your 401(k) plan or other workplace savings plan to reduce your income taxes.

If your debt is under control, and you're ready to start investing, consider using your employer's retirement savings plan such as a 401(k), 403(b), or 457 plan. You can likely achieve diversification using mutual funds or similar investments that are commonly available under these plans. Some employers will even match a part of your contribution. In addition to increasing your savings, you'll reduce your current taxable income, which, in turn, reduces the amount of federal (and possibly state or other) income taxes you'll owe.

54

If you run a business, full-time or part-time, always report your earnings to the IRS.

There is no excuse for failing to report income to the IRS and, if necessary, to your state or other tax authorities. Remember, someone who gets paid under the table is still getting paid. Taxpayers must comply with the law or risk severe consequences for filing falsified tax returns.

INSURANCE

Insurance is possibly the least exciting subject in personal finance. Don't think of it as a necessary evil. Understand it for what it is— your protection against catastrophic loss.

55
Get insurance coverage for your business, even your part-time business.

Many homeowners insurance policies exclude liability coverage for any activity that earns any amount of money, no matter how small. Trying to reduce your insurance bill, by pretending you're not earning money in your small home-based business, will likely fail. Don't get left without liability coverage. Many businesses can get adequate coverage for a lower premium than you might expect. Ask your insurance provider for information on the type of coverage appropriate to your business.

56
Beware of day-care providers paid under the table.

If your day-care provider is paid without a paper trail, chances are the provider is not properly insured in case your child gets injured. Remember, many homeowners insurance policies don't cover activity that produces any income, no matter how small. Expecting your day-care provider to be able to fool the insurance company is courting disaster. You don't want to risk having no money available to cover costs for potentially crippling injuries to your child because of an uninsured day-care provider.

57
To verify the coverage carried by your day-care provider, go to the source: the insurer.

Speak to your day-care provider's insurer directly or ask the provider to have the insurer prepare a certificate of insurance, indicating that the day-care service is covered. While this option isn't as good as reviewing the insurance policy, it's one helpful step in a system that has no perfect method for verifying insurance coverage.

58
Offer to pay your day-care provider's increased cost of insurance coverage.

Some homeowner's policies can be endorsed to provide day-care coverage for $50 to $180 a year. Offer to add one to four dollars a week to your day-care provider's fee to cover the cost of adequate insurance coverage.

59
Give careful thought to how much life insurance you need.

Don't expect the rules of thumb, such as a multiple of your income, to tell you how much life insurance to buy. If this formula works, it's a lucky coincidence. Instead, use real life insurance calculators like those found on the "Choose to Save" website at www.ChooseToSave.org.

60
Consider buying long-term care insurance while you are still young.

If you buy long-term care insurance when you're in your forties instead of your sixties, you will not only pay a lower annual premium based on your age, but you'll eliminate twenty years of possible illness or injury that might make you uninsurable. You may also qualify for an entire classification of lower rates because your health is probably better now than it will be when you're older.

61
Try to get adequate uninsured and underinsured motorist coverage.

This kind of insurance covers pain and suffering, lost wages, medical bills, and other expenses that should be the responsibility of an uninsured, at-fault driver who rarely has money to cover legal liabilities in case of an accident. Coverage of this kind isn't available everywhere—shop around if you're having trouble finding uninsured and underinsured motorist coverage.

62
Buy an umbrella liability policy to raise your coverage limits.

An umbrella policy raises your liability coverage from, for example, $300,000 to $1,000,000 on both your homeowners and automobile insurance policies, in case you are sued by someone harmed in an accident. The cost is often less than $250 a year.

63

Make sure you have coverage in case of disability.

Disability insurance pays you if you can't go to work because you're sick or you're injured. Before you retire, you're probably more likely to become disabled than you are to die. Even so, life insurance is common among Americans while disability coverage is far less so. You may be able to get disability insurance through your employer, professional association, or life insurance provider.

64

Use your healthy eating and exercise program to save money on insurance coverage.

As your health improves, you may find you qualify for better coverage or lower rates on medical, disability, long-term care, and life insurance. All these coverages take your health into consideration in their rate structure, and in the insurer's willingness to cover you at all. It also doesn't hurt to ask what policy choices might result in a lower premium.

ESTATE PLANNING

*Most of us need not worry about estate taxes.
Instead, it may be best to focus on the basics
of estate planning. It takes only a few steps (and the
help of qualified legal counsel) to make life easier for
those who have to make important decisions
when we can't speak for ourselves.*

65
Buy a trust only if you need one.

A trust can be used as an alternative to a will and other estate planning tools. But trusts can be costly to set up, and may require frequent revision. Many trusts (especially living trusts) are sold to people who don't actually need them. Whether or not you need a trust can be a matter of opinion, depending on many factors. If a trust is reccommended to you, be sure you clearly understand and agree with the need for it, especially if it's suggested as a replacement for having a simple will.

66
Have your will made or updated.

If you die without a will, a probate court cannot acknowledge your wishes (even if you wrote them in some other form) and would have to distribute your assets as set forth by law. If you care about what happens to your property when you die, make a will—or have your existing will updated—to reflect your wishes.

67
Get legal help to prepare your will.

While stationery store forms and computer programs claim to make wills that are legal in every state, experience shows that courts won't always recognize them. For a document as important as this, do you really want to use the cut-rate option and risk your wishes not being honored?

68
Review your will every two years (or sooner if you have a major change in your life) and revise it as often as necessary.

The beauty of a typical will is that it has absolutely no meaning until you die, and then becomes so ironclad at your passing that it will thereafter be enforced by a court of law. Don't hesitate to change your will if circumstances in your life call for it.

69
Consider getting a durable power of attorney so someone can sign documents for you if you are unavailable or incapacitated.

If you don't have a durable power of attorney, a court can appoint a guardian for you if you become incompetent. However, this is often costly and time-consuming. If you need someone to look after your affairs, a durable power of attorney can be an inexpensive alternative. Be sure to complete the arrangements ahead of time before the need arises.

70
Be cautious whom you appoint to act for you under your durable power of attorney.

A durable power of attorney is a "blank check" that will typically allow your designee (called your agent or "attorney-in-fact") to *clean you out*. That person could have the power, for instance, to empty all your bank accounts and sell your house out from under you. To be prudent, you may want to consider giving this authority only to a spouse or a blood relative.

71
Understand the difference between a will and a power of attorney.

Your will has no effect while you live, but takes effect at your death. A power of attorney can be used to have someone act for you while you live, but becomes useless when you die.

72
Have medical proxies prepared.

In some states, medical proxies are called health care proxies or health care powers of attorney. These are used in addition to a living will and are recommended to most people who want a living will. Living wills and medical proxies are collectively called

Advance Directives =
living Will + Medical power of Atty

"advance directives" because they offer guidance on patient health care before the need arises.

73

Understand the difference between medical proxies and a durable power of attorney.

No matter what name they go by, medical proxies are usually limited to medical matters while a durable power of attorney may be limited to financial and business matters. Lawyers often recommend that the two should not overlap. If you want a durable power of attorney to qualify as a medical proxy, consult with qualified legal counsel.

74

Understand the difference between living wills and medical proxies.

A living will can express your wish not to be kept alive by heroic measures (typically if you are in a persistent vegetative state), but by themselves, living wills aren't always honored. Medical proxies appoint someone to act on your behalf in medical matters, including the crucial task of hiring and firing physicians. If your doctor won't respect your wishes under the terms of your living will, your agent under your medical proxy can typically replace that physician with one who will carry out your stated wishes.

SAVING FOR COLLEGE, INVESTING FOR RETIREMENT

College and retirement are two of the most costly goals you may ever pursue. But how can you prepare for both at the same time? Whether you're considering college funding and investing for retirement for the first time, or you've been working on these goals for years, remember these important points.

75

Save for your own retirement before saving for your children's college.

It's generally a lot easier to use excess retirement funds to pay for your child's college than to use excess college funds to pay for your retirement. Many advisors point out that you have a limited amount of time to save for retirement, while your children will have their entire working lives to pay off their student loans. Perhaps the best gift you can give your children is the assurance that they won't have to support you in your old age. And if you happen to save more than you need for retirement, you can always help your children pay off their student loans. (Meanwhile, your savings will have had more time to grow.)

76

Keep savings for your child in your own name, not in your child's name or in a custodial account, for a better financial aid award.

If you're trying to decide whether to keep $1,000 of your child's college money in your name or your child's, look at the effect on college financial aid. One common formula reduces the student's financial aid award by 35 percent ($350 per $1,000) of the money in the student's name. Money in the parents' names will reduce the award by less than 6 percent ($60 per $1,000). Remember that money in custodial accounts—Uniform Gift to Minors Act (UGMA) and Uniform Transfers to Minors Act (UTMA) accounts—will be considered the child's in their financial aid calculation. Having the money in your name may mean a bigger financial aid award for your college-bound child.

77
Consult an experienced college planner as early as you can.

If you begin the college planning process when your child enters high school, you will have more time to examine a variety of techniques that can maximize benefits to you and your child. Hiring a fee-only college planner—one who isn't trying to sell you investments—will pose fewer conflicts of interest than working with those who want to sell you annuities, life insurance, or IRAs.

78
Don't assume a state college or university will be your least expensive option for higher education. Check into private schools, too.

Some private schools offer tuition discounts, especially for high-performing students. Taking advantage of incentives that state schools may not offer might reduce the total cost of a private school education to less than the cost of attending a state school.

79
Consider more than financial aid and the student's ability to gain admission when selecting the right college; you want the best match.

Your goal is to find the best match between what the school offers and what the student needs. Just because a certain college will admit your child doesn't mean that school will provide the best learning or living environment for him or her. Avoid experiencing the frustration—and expense—that can come from choosing a college that's a bad fit for your child's education and future.

80
Have your child apply for every scrap of financial aid he or she might possibly qualify for.

In addition to federal or school-based aid, financial aid awards are available from many civic and social organizations. Your child's guidance counselor, the college's financial aid office, or an experienced college planner can help you identify hard-to-find sources of financial aid.

81
Start making investments as early in your life as possible.

Whether it's for your kids' college, your own retirement, or some other goal, remember that when you invest, you're investing two things: one is *money*; the other is *time*. To reach any investment goal, the more you have of one, the less you need of the other.

82
Understand the limitations of investments.

Because investing in the stock market is a long-term financial technique, it should be kept in its proper perspective. It's important to understand you can't invest your way out of financial problems such as having inadequate insurance coverage or spending beyond your means.

83
Keep cash equivalents accessible for your immediate needs.

The money you need for your immediate living expenses—your "I don't need credit cards" money— should stay in highly stable accounts, such as money market accounts or FDIC-insured bank accounts. Put emergency funds into Certificates of Deposit (CDs). You may wonder whether CDs are liquid enough for emergencies. But with CDs, you'll be less tempted to spend the money, and you may earn a little more interest than with bank accounts. If you do need the money for a true emergency, the amount of the early withdrawal penalty is usually inconsequential in comparison.

84
Put your emergency fund into a "CD ladder" to minimize early withdrawal penalties.

Instead of putting, say, $20,000 into one two-year CD, split it up into four CDs of $5,000 each, maturing in six, twelve, eighteen, and twenty-four months. As each CD matures, re-deposit it into a new *two-year* CD. Then make sure all four CDs are set up to automatically roll over at maturity for another two years. Now you'll have $20,000 (plus interest) growing for you at two-year rates, with $5,000 available every six months. And if you do need to withdraw money for a $5,000 emergency, you'll pay an early withdrawal penalty on only one quarter of your emergency fund.

85
Don't exceed your own tolerance for risk when investing.

With investments, there's no chance of reward without at least an equal risk. If you would be heartbroken to ever lose any of your money, stick to FDIC-insured bank accounts. Better still, educate yourself about investment risks so you can take appropriate amounts of risk wisely.

86
Consider putting aggressive growth investments into Roth accounts.

A Roth IRA and Roth 401(k) are different from other retirement accounts. The money that goes into a Roth account does not give you any immediate tax benefit, but over time it can grow *tax-free*. This means that if you can get $3,000 of investment to grow to $10,000 in value, you'll have $7,000 of earnings on which you will never be taxed. Ask your tax advisor about the rules of Roth accounts.

87
Think of a capital gain as your *friend.*

If you sell investments that have increased in value, unless they're in a tax-deferred account like an IRA or 401(k), you'll likely owe tax on this gain. People hate to pay this capital gains tax, partly because they usually have to write a check to the IRS to do it. Actually, on ordinary long-term investments, capital gains tax rates are *lower* than the tax rate you pay on the income that you earn at your job or business.

88
Pay your capital gains taxes as soon as you make a taxable sale.

Doing so reduces the chance of an underpayment penalty when you file your return. This also keeps you from spending the money you should have set aside for the tax liability. Write checks to the IRS and any other applicable taxing authorities, and send them as soon as you have the proceeds from the sale. Remember, even if income tax is withheld from the proceeds, that amount isn't always enough. Consult your tax advisor.

89
Use mutual funds for your equity investments.

Most of us don't have the time to properly analyze individual stocks or the money to diversify them adequately. Many mutual fund investments give you a low-cost way to make sure your money is professionally managed and diversified.

90
Understand that not all mutual funds are the same.

While two funds might be similar to one another, other mutual funds are as individual as fingerprints. Make sure you understand exactly what fund you're investing in and whether it's right for you.

91
Screen your mutual funds for low expenses.

The more the mutual fund company takes to cover its expenses, the less money is left in the fund for you. This means that among similar funds (investing in similar assets), the fund that has the lowest expenses will likely give you the highest return in the long run. Do the homework. A little research on expenses could save you a lot of money.

92
Draft and sign an Investment Policy Statement.

An Investment Policy Statement is a personalized document that describes why you are investing and how you intend to go about it. It often includes asset allocations (what percentage of your investments belong in which categories), reasons for investing the way you do, objectives for your investments, and a statement that you'll follow the investment policy in times of market turbulence. Use it to help you see whether the next investment you may make heads you in the right direction for your overall plan.

93
Put aside enough emergency cash.

It can be tempting to take your emergency funds and put them in the stock market, but don't do it. You could lose your emergency savings. Remember, your equities, including mutual funds that own stocks, may be the engine of your financial vehicle, but your emergency fund is your *air bag*. Sometimes an emergency starts as a meltdown in the stock market. Just like with an air bag, by the time you see the crash coming, it's too late to set up your emergency fund.

BONUS TIPS

*Your money, and your money problems,
can sometimes seem overwhelming.
Remember to keep everything in perspective.*

1
Make money your servant, not your master.

You may have heard that "he who dies with the most toys wins." But that's not true. He who dies with the most toys is *dead*. What's important is what you do with your *life*. Strive to make money your ally in creating a better life, so you can experience more joy, peace, love, contentment, and fulfillment.

2
Start small, but get started!

Sure, there may be a lot of steps you feel you should take to get better control of your finances. Choose just one or two to get started. Begin by asking yourself what you can do in the next thirty minutes to improve your financial life and repeat that question every day for a week. This may not sound like much, but remember what Lao Tsu said about the journey of a thousand miles. Take small steps, and you'll probably make more progress in one week than you've made in the past year. Eventually, your money worries will diminish. And the moment you stop worrying about money, life gets better.

WHAT'S YOUR FAVORITE FINANCIAL TIP?

Has a tip in this book helped you improve your life?

Do you have a favorite tip of your own?

Tell us about it at:

www.FinancialTipsBook.com

All submissions become the property of
The Kenneth Robinson Company and
may be used in future editions.

Action Steps:

_____

_____

_____

_____

_____

_____

_____

_____

_____

_____

_____

_____

_____

_____

_____

_____

_____

_____

_____

_____

_____

_____

_____

_____

Action Steps:

_____

_____

_____

_____

_____

_____

_____

_____

_____

_____

_____

_____

_____

_____

_____

_____

_____

_____

_____

_____

_____

Action Steps:

_____

_____

_____

_____

_____

_____

_____

_____

_____

_____

_____

_____

_____

_____

_____

_____

_____

_____

_____

_____

_____

_____

_____

_____

ABOUT THE AUTHOR

Kenneth F. Robinson, JD, CFP® is a professional speaker, financial planner, and
money coach who says, "The moment you stop
worrying about money, life gets better."

A member of the National Speakers Association, the Alliance of Cambridge Advisors, and the
National Association of Personal Financial Advisors, Ken is a frequent presenter on personal finance
for people who work for a living or are retired from
working for a living.

Ken is a Certified Financial Planner™ designee, and has been quoted in *Kiplinger's Personal
Finance*, MSN's MoneyCentral.com, and Cleve-
land's *The Plain Dealer*.

Ken sells no investment or insurance products. He is the founder of Practical Financial Planning and The Kenneth Robinson Company.

Schedule Ken Robinson to speak at your next meeting or event. His programs include:

- *Don't Make a Budget! Why It's So Hard to Save Money, and What To Do About It*
- *Faith and Finance*
- *Overcoming Financial Dysfunction: How to Make Better Decisions About Money*
- *Financial Calm in a Time of Change*

Ken also provides individual cash flow coaching and leads the Personal Finance Reading Club, a discussion group for people reading important works on personal finance.

For more information or additional copies of *Financial Tips for a Better Life,* call toll free 877.536.8020 or visit:

www.KennethRobinson.com.